A Family Christmas Celebration Arranged for Choirs of All Ages

by TOM FETTKE

LILLENAS

lillenas.com

Contents

Detailed table of contents found on page 144

I
The Light of the World

Adult Choir, Child (or Student) Solo, Narrator

Arranged by Tom Fettke

CD: 2
Faster ♩ = ca. 80
*"Shine Your Light"
Child Solo (Female adult or older student)
mp
14
Shine Your light of
come.
G sus
Faster
G
F/G
G
C
hope,
Shine Your light of peace,
G/B
Gm6/B♭
B♭6
A7sus
A7
A7♭9
18
CD: 3
Shine Your light of love and joy,
Shine Your light on
Dm7
G sus
G/F
Em7
Am7
Dm7
Dm/C

rit.
23
a tempo
mf
us.
Shine Your light of
Choir
Divisi mp
Oo
Divisi mp
B♭
G sus
G
F/G
G
23
C
rit.
cresc.
mf a tempo
hope,
Shine Your light of peace,
G/B
Gm6/B♭
B♭6
A7sus
A7
A7♭9

27
rit.
Shine Your light of love and joy, Shine Your
Oo
27
Dm7
Gsus
G
F
Em7
Am7
Dm7
rit.
a tempo
light on us.
Gsus
G
F
G
A♭
D♭
A♭
a tempo

CD: 4

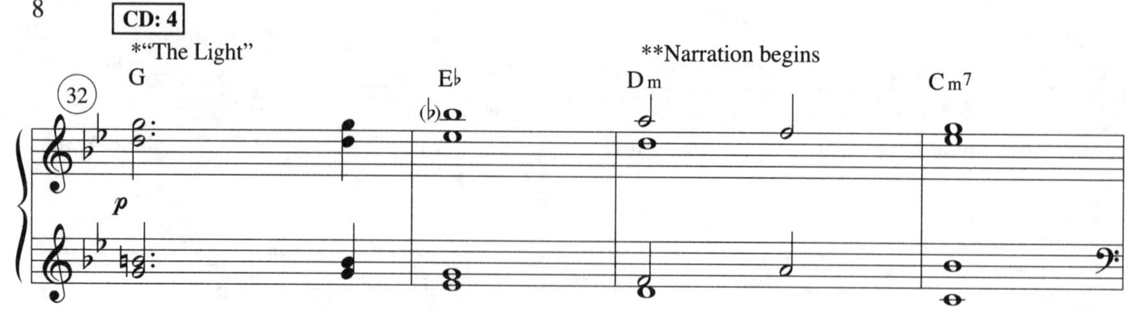

**NARRATOR: The Word became a human being and lived among us, and we saw His glory, the glory that is His, as the only Son of the Father, full of grace and truth…

All that came to be had life in Him; and this life gives light to all mankind, a light that shines in the darkness–and the darkness can never put it out. And to all those who believe in the Light He gives the right to become children of God.

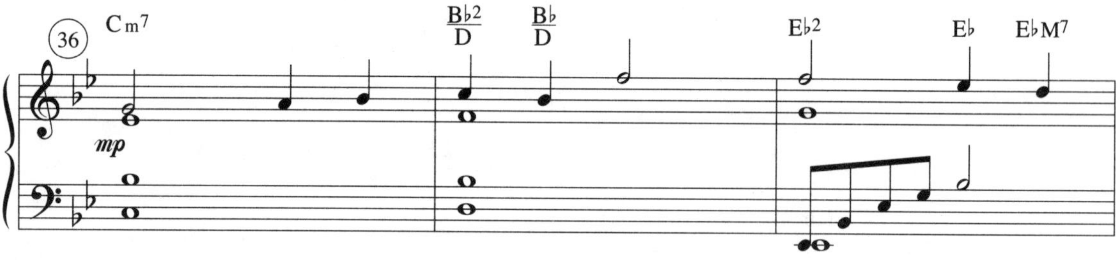

36 Cm7 B♭2/D B♭/D E♭2 E♭ E♭M7

mp

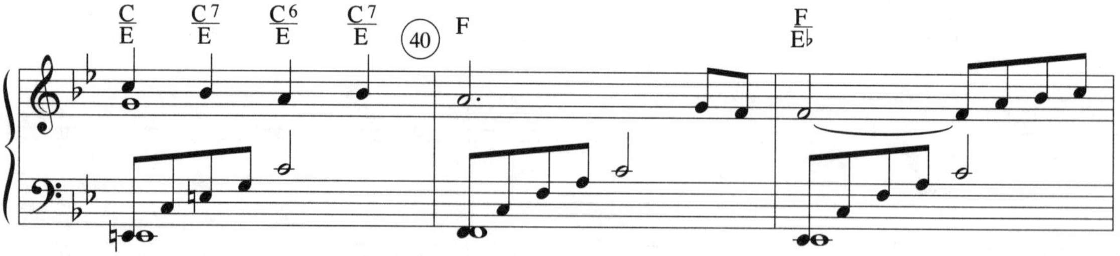

C/E C7/E C6/E C7/E 40 F F/E♭

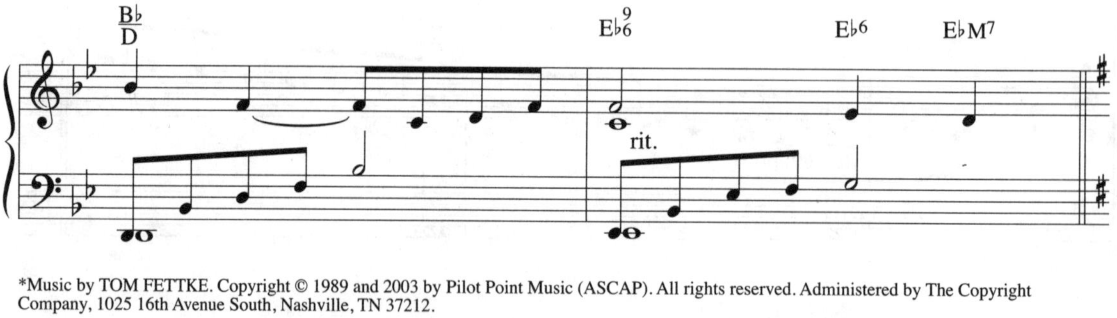

B♭/D E♭6/9 E♭6 E♭M7

rit.

*Music by TOM FETTKE.

*Words and Music by TOM FETTKE. Administered by The Copyright Company, 1025 16th Avenue South, Nashville, TN 37212.

57
He is the Fa-ther of lights,
verse re - veals, His bright-est star now shines; For
C CM7 Dsus D
C/G G C6/G G C/G G Am/G G
CD: 6
He is the Fa - ther of the Light of the World. He is the
C G2/B Am7 Dsus D
62
Fa-ther of Lights, The Fa-ther of lights,
Fa-ther of Lights, He is the great Cre - a - tor. The u - ni -
C/G G C6/G G C/G G Am/G G C/G G C6/G G

66

He is the Fa-ther of lights,

verse re - veals, His bright-est star now shines; For

C CM7 Dsus D 66 C/G G C6/G G C/G G Am/G G

CD: 7

decresc.

He is the Fa - ther of the Light of the World.

decresc.

C G2/B Am7 D13 D7 G G/F

decresc.

Unison ***mf*** 72

The Word be - came flesh and lived a -

Unison ***mf***

E♭ 72 A♭ B♭/A♭

mf

76
mong us, And we have seen the
Gm7 Cm7 Fm7 76 B♭m7
glo - ry of the Lord. He
E♭7 D♭/E♭ E♭ A♭2 D♭2/A♭
80 Divisi
came to shine light in the dark -
Divisi
80 A♭ A♭4/2 A♭ G♭/A♭ A♭ G♭/A♭ A♭7 F/A

CD: 8
84
cresc.
ness, So the lost could be-come chil - dren of
cresc.
B♭m
A♭/E♭
D♭ D♭M7 D♭6
B♭2/D
B♭/D
cresc.
f
88
God. He is the
Fa-ther of Lights,
Fa-ther of Lights, He is the
E♭sus
E♭
D♭/A♭ A♭ D♭6/A♭ A♭
f
The Fa-ther of lights, He is the
great Cre - a - tor. The u - ni - verse re - veals,
D♭/A♭ A♭ B♭m/A♭ A♭
D♭/A♭ A♭ D♭6/A♭ A♭
D♭ D♭M7 E♭sus E♭

92
Fa-ther of lights,
His bright-est star now shines;
For He is the Fa - ther of the
D♭/A♭ A♭ D♭6/A♭ A♭
D♭/A♭ A♭ B♭m/A♭ A♭
D♭ A♭2/C
Light of the World.
He is the
97
Fa-ther of Lights,
Fa-ther of Lights, He is the
B♭m7 E♭sus E♭
D♭/A♭ A♭ D♭6/A♭ A♭
The Fa-ther of lights,
He is the
great Cre - a - tor.
The u-ni-verse re - veals,
D♭/A♭ A♭ B♭m/A♭ A♭
D♭/A♭ A♭ D♭6/A♭ A♭
D♭ D♭M7 E♭sus E♭

*Sing cued notes if bass range is too high.

111
(,)
up your voice! For He will shine for - ev - er and for -
Bbm
Fm
Gb
111
rit.
fff
115
ev - er! Re - joice!
Absus
Ab
115
Db
rit.
Db
Db
rit.
8vb

II
Shine Your Light of Hope

Adult Choir, Opt. Adult Solo, Narrator

Arranged by Tom Fettke

*Words and Music by TOM GRASSI and TOM FETTKE. Copyright © 2003 by Pilot Point Music (ASCAP). Administered by The Copyright Company, 1025 16th Avenue South, Nashville, TN 37212.

10
world that the Christ has come.
Child to be crowned my King.
D♭M7
B♭m7
E♭7sus
A♭2
D♭6 9/A♭
E♭7/A♭
14
Once a si - lence, now a voice.
Once de - feat - ed, now there's hope.
cresc.
18
Once a still - ness, now re - joic - ing in heav - en with a
Once a dis - cord, now com - posed is a song of per - fect
A♭
A♭7
E♭m7
D♭2
cresc.

2nd time to Coda
(to pg. 21, meas. 42)
CD: 11
song my heart can sing,
praise. So let us
B♭2/D
B♭/D
Gm/B♭
D♭6/E♭
E♭sus
E♭
D♭/E♭
E♭

22
Unison f
Glo - ry to God!
Al - le - lu -
Unison f
A♭
E♭/G
Fm
Fm/E♭
D♭M7
Cm7
f

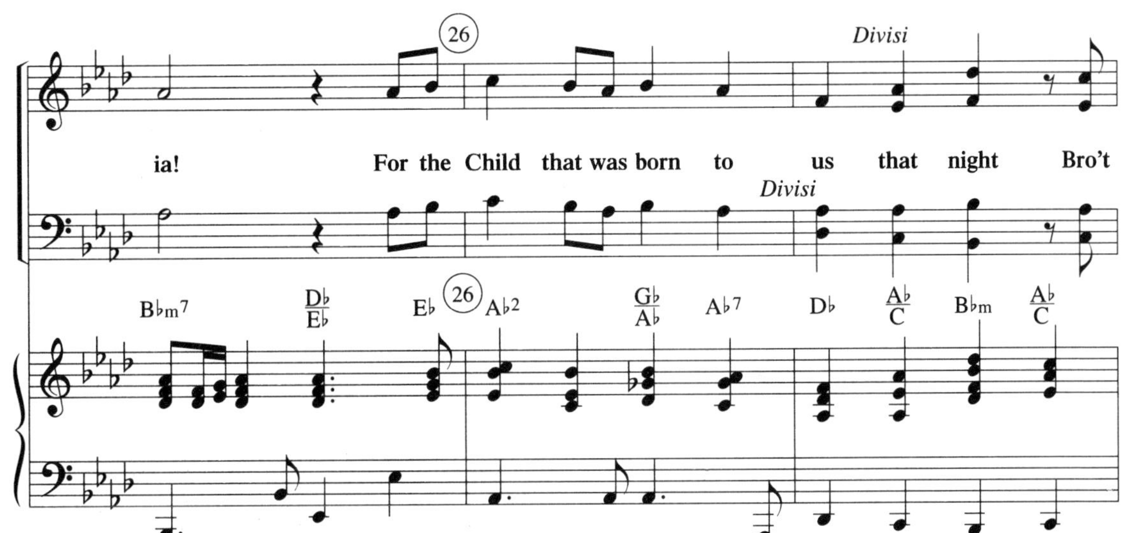
26
Divisi
ia!
For the Child that was born to us that night Bro't
Divisi
B♭m7
D♭/E♭
E♭
A♭2
G♭/A♭
A♭7
D♭
A♭/C
B♭m
A♭/C

30
Unison
heav - en down to earth.
Glo - ry to
Unison
D♭ D♭M7 B♭/D Fm/D E♭sus E♭
30
A♭ E♭/G
God!
Al - le - lu - ia!
Come and
Fm Fm/E♭ D♭M7 Cm7 B♭m7 D♭/E♭ E♭
34
Divisi
wor - ship the Ev - er - last - ing Light,
And
Divisi
A♭ A♭4/2 G♭/A♭ A♭7 D♭6 A♭/C B♭m D♭m6/B♭
34

38
rit.
a tempo
cel - e-brate His ho - ly birth.
A♭/E♭ A♭M7/E♭ A♭/E♭ D♭6/E♭ D♭/E♭ A♭sus A♭
CD: 12
rit.
D.S. al Coda
(to pg. 17, meas. 6)
CD: 13
CODA
sing,
B♭m A♭/B♭ B♭m/A♭ E♭7sus E♭7 D♭6/E♭
44
a tempo
Unison f
Glo - ry to God!
E sus E D/E E A E/G♯ F♯m F♯m/E
f a tempo

48
Al - le - lu - ia! For the Child that was born to
D M7 C♯m7 B m7 D2/E E A2 G/A A7
48
Divisi
us that night Bro't heav - en down to earth.
Divisi
D A/C♯ B m A/C♯ D D M7 B/D♯ F♯m/D♯ E sus E
52
Unison
Glo - ry to God! Al - le - lu -
Unison
52
A E/G♯ F♯m F♯m/E D M7 C♯m7

(56) *Divisi*

ia! Come and wor - ship the Ev - er -

Divisi

Bm7 D/E E (56) A A4/2 A G/A A7

last - ing Light, And cel - e-brate His

D6 A/C♯ Bm Dm6/B A AM7/E A/E

(60) decresc.

ho - ly birth.

decresc.

(60) D6/E D/E A sus A

decresc.

CD: 14

*Music by TOM FETTKE, GEORGE F. HANDEL, JOHN FRANCIS WADE and EMMY KOHLER.

*NARRATOR: "And now, the mystery, which remained hidden for ages and generations, has been revealed to God's people. Through them God has chosen to make known how rich and glorious it is. The mystery we speak of is this; Christ in you, the hope of glory." *(Colossians 1:25-27, para.)*

Joseph and Mary were people of hope. When God called them, He called them to take a risk…a risk that disrupted their plans and threatened their reputations and their lives. But because of their hope they could take the risk that faith requires. They believed all God's promises–the promise that a virgin would give birth to a son…the promise that this son, Jesus, would be called the Son of God and would bring salvation to all people…the promise of Emmanuel, that God would be with us.

God calls us to be a people of hope. As we dispel the darkness by lighting this candle, remember that hope is not a ship at the mercy of prevailing winds. It is an anchor of the soul, firm and secure, that penetrates the deep invisible places of the heart of God.

(If the candle lighting cermony isn't used, substitute the following paragraph)

God calls us to be a people of hope. Remember that our hope is not a ship at the mercy of prevailing winds. It is an anchor of the soul, firm and secure, that penetrates the deep invisible places of the heart of God.

FM7
Dm9
82
D♭
G♭M7
G♭6
rit.
Fsus
F
85
B♭2
a tempo
Gm4 7
E♭M7
A♭2/C
B♭2/D
C2/E
90
F
C/E
B♭/D
F2/C
B♭
Gm7/C
C/B♭
F2/A
F/A
Gm4 7
C/B♭
94
F2/A
F/A
Gm7
C7/G
CD: 15
Faster ♩ = ca. 80
F
Dm
B♭2
Gm7
C2
C
Gm7/C
C7
rit.
Fsus

*Words by TOM FETTKE; Music by JOHN F. WADE.

107
Bow down be - fore Him, Wor - ship and a -
107
F/A Gm7/4 F Gm7/4 C7 F C/E F Dm G2/B
Unison
111
dore Him For He a - lone is wor - thy, For
Unison
C Dm/C C B♭/C 111 F/C C F/C Gm/C F/C
115
He a - lone is wor - thy, For He a - lone is
F/C C F/C B♭/C F/C C/B♭ F/A 115 Gm7 F/A Gm/B♭ Dm/B

*Words and Music by GRAHAM KENDRICK.

126
Divisi
mel.
an - gel song, For our Cre - a - tor be - comes our Sav - ior,
B♭M7 Csus C Dm Dm/C B♭ C B♭
Unison
130
as a ba - by born! Heav - en and earth bow in
Gm7 Csus C F2(no 3)
a - dor - a - tion; "Glo - ry to God in the high - est heav'n!"
F2(no 3) F2 Dm11 Csus B♭M7 Csus C
134
Divisi
CD: 17
mel.
Send the good news out to ev - 'ry na - tion, For our hope is
Dm Dm/C B♭ C B♭ Gm7

138
Divisi
f
born.
Wor - ship the King! See His bright - ness;
Divisi f
C sus
A
C♯
138
D m
f
G m7
C
C6
142
Unison
Wor - ship the King, His won - ders tell: Je - sus our King is
Unison
D m
G m7
C
142
D m
D m
C
born to - day– We wel - come You, Em - man - u -
G m
B♭
C
G m7
B♭2
C
C7

146
CD: 18
el!
146
F2(no 3)
F2
G♭2(no 3)
E♭m11
150
Won - der-ful, Coun - sel - or, Might - y God,
Men unison f
C♭M7
D♭sus
D♭
G♭2(no 3)
150
154
Fa - ther for - ev - er, the Prince of Peace;
There is no end to Your
Divisi
mel.
E♭m11
D♭sus
C♭M7
D♭sus
D♭
154
E♭m
E♭m
D♭

rule of jus - tice, It will nev - er cease.
Unison
C♭ D♭ C♭ A♭m7 D♭sus D♭
158
Light of Your face come to pierce the dark - ness; Joy of Your heart come to
G♭2 E♭m11
chase the gloom; Star of the morn - ing, a new day dawn - ing,
162
Divisi
mel.
C♭M7 D♭sus D♭ E♭m C♭ D♭ C♭

CD: 19
Make our hearts Your home.
Unison
A♭m7
D♭sus
D♭
Dsus
D
decresc.
167
Unison
mp
Qui - et - ly He came as a help - less Ba - by–
G2(no 3)
G2
One day in pow'r He will come a - gain;
sub. f
Em11
Dsus
C9/6
Dsus
D

171
Divisi
When thro' the skies He will burst with splen - dor
Divisi
171
Em
Em
D
C
D
C
Unison
175
on the earth to reign. Je - sus, we bow at Your
Unison
Am7
Dsus
D
175
G
detached
man - ger low - ly; Now let Your will in our
G
G2
G
Em7

179
Divisi
lives be done; Live in my flesh by Your
Divisi
CM7
Dsus
D
179
Em
Em
D
CD: 20
Spir - it ho - ly till Your King - dom comes.
C
D
C
Am7
Am6
Am7
Dsus
B
D♯
183
Wor - ship the King, Come, see His bright - ness; Wor - ship the King, His
183
Em
Am
D
D6
Em

187
Unison
wonders tell: Jesus our King is born today– We
Unison
Am7
D
187
Em
Em/D
Am/C
D
D6
CD: 21
2nd time
1
welcome You, Emmanuel!
Am7
C2/D
D7
1
G2(no 3)
Em11
(to pg. 36, meas. 183)
2
cresc.
el!
cresc.
(to pg. 36, meas. 183)
2
C9/6
Dsus
B/D#
G
more legato
cresc.

195
Divisi
ff
Joy to the world! Our hope
Divisi
ff
G/D
Am/D
G/D
Am/D
G/D
199
has come!
D
G2(no 3)
detached
Em11
C9/6
D
G

III
Shine Your Light of Peace

Adult Choir, Student or Young Adult Soloist, Youth Choir or Praise Team and Narrator

Arranged by Tom Fettke

Fill-ing the Beth - le-hem sky. The
Fill-ing the Beth - le-hem sky. A -
Am
FM7
Em7
11
shep - herds watched in a - maze - ment,
mazed that they had been cho - sen
11
Am
Em
G
FM7
The heav - ens burn - ing like fire.
To hear the heav - en - ly choir.
C
G
G7sus
G

15

And as the light grew bright - er
And when the song had fad - ed

15 C G/B

They heard a great and glo - ri - ous song From
A joy re-placed their lin - ger - ing fear. They

C/B♭ F2/A F/A F

19

an - gels des - cend - ing from heav -
ran to the birth - place of Je -

19 Am FM7 C/G

CD: 23 1st time
CD: 25 2nd time
en,
A mess - age of love and hope so
sus
With glo - ry still ring - ing in their
Am/F♯
C/G
rit.
Unison f
24
a tempo
strong.
ears.
Peace on earth, good-will to
F/G
G
F/G
G7
C2
C
rit.
a tempo
men,
The Sav - ior sleeps in Beth - le -
F2
F
C/G
F2/G
G

28 *Divisi*

hem; And on this won - 'drous night He

Divisi

C 28 F F2 G/F

brings His light, And His King - dom shall not

C/E Am7 C/D D7 D9

rit. *Unison* 32 a tempo

end. The an - gels sang, their prais - es

Unison

F/G G F/G G7 32 C2 C

rit. a tempo

Divisi
rang To pro - claim the Ba - by's
Divisi
F2 F E E7sus/F♯ E7/G♯
36
birth. He has come, God's love - ly
Am FM7 36 C/G
1 CD: 24
(to pg. 39, meas. 7)
decresc.
Son, Peace on earth.
decresc.
F6/G Em/G G7 1C
(to pg. 39, meas. 7)
decresc.

*Words by JOHN S. DWIGHT; Music by ADOLPHE C. ADAM. Arr. © 2003 by Pilot Point Music (ASCAP). All rights reserved. Administered by The Copyright Company, 1025 16th Avenue South, Nashville, TN 37212.

vine! O night when Christ was born!
C/E F G/F F C/G G7 C
50
O night! O ho - ly
(,)
Csus/D C/E G G/F C/E F2 FM7
night when Christ was born! Christ was
C/G G F/G G7 C

54

rit.

born! Peace on earth! A - men.

D/C Ab/C Bb/C

rit.

a tempo

rit.

C C/G Gm9 C C/G Gm9 C

a tempo

rit.

8vb

CD: 27

With anticipation ♩ = ca. 76 N.C. 60 *"Light of Peace"

mp

*Music by RICHARD S. WILLIS and GEORGE FREDERICK HANDEL.

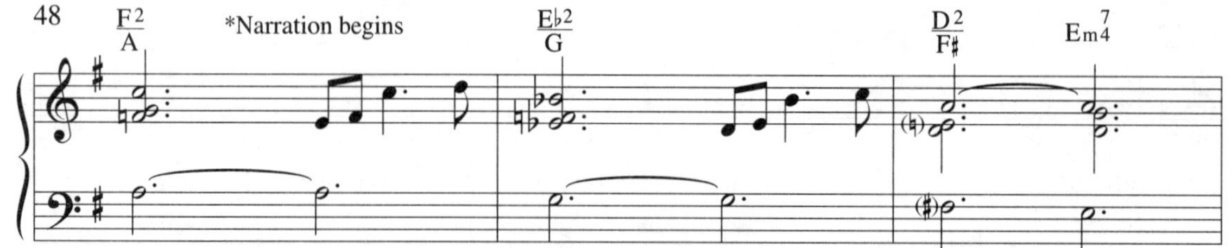

*NARRATOR: Zechariah, the father of John the Baptist, prayed that God would send the Morning Star from heaven to shine on those living in darkness and guide them into the path of peace.

The Morning Star was born in Bethlehem. When Mary gave birth to Jesus a host of angels filled the night sky with light…and a song of praise echoed across the heavens. "Peace on earth…peace to everyone whom God blesses." God's perfect peace had arrived… peace between God and us…a peace that is deep and unshakeable, a peace that surpasses all understanding, bringing comfort to the human heart.

As we light this candle, may we treasure the perfect peace God gives to His people: "For to us a child is born, to us a son is given, and the government will be on his shoulders. And he will be called Wonderful Counselor, Mighty God, Everlasting Father, Prince of Peace." *(Isaiah 9:6)*

If the candle lighting ceremony is not used, substitute this paragraph:

This Christmas may we treasure the perfect peace God gives His people: "For to us a child is born, to us a son is given, and the government will be on his shoulders. And he will be called Wonderful Counselor, Mighty God, Everlasting Father, Prince of Peace." *(Isaiah 9:6)*

Much faster ♩ = ca. 132
Bm7
B♭7
Am7
D7
rit.
73
Gsus
G
C
A7/C♯
77
D
B7/D♯
Em
C/E
81
Dsus
D
Bsus
B
cresc.
85
Em
mf
CD: 28
Student (or young adult) solo
mf
His
Em
Bm7
Em
Am/E

*Words by KEN BIBLE and TOM FETTKE; Music adapted from plainsong by THOMAS HELMORE.

CD: 29

cresc. *f*

He ___ is might. ___ Em -

Am Bm/D D Gsus G

cresc.

(105)

man - u - el, Em - man - u - el. His

D/F♯ Em Bm/D Am/C Am7 B B7/D♯ Em Em/D D

f

(109)

decresc. *mf*

name is called Em - man - u - el, Em-man-u -

CM7 G6/B Am6 Em/B Bm7

decresc.

(114) CD: 30

el.

C Fm E♭

mf

*Words and Music by DAVID ALLEN FETTKE.

126
Divisi
mel.
Bless-ed Child, He was born to
E♭/D♭
Fm
E♭
save us,
Prince of Peace, Might-y
130
D♭M7
CD: 31
cresc.
f
God, the Mes - si - ah. The Mes-

Student (or young adult) Solo
134
f
Lord of lords, Son of God, Prince of Peace, Might-y
si - ah, The Mes - si - ah,
134
Fm
B♭/F
Fm
f
God, The Mes - si - ah.
138
He is the Mes-
B♭/F
138
F♯m

142
He's the Won-der-ful Coun - sel - or, He's the In - fi - nite
si - ah. The Mes - si - ah,
F♯m
B
F♯
142
F♯m
CD: 32
Soloist may sing melody with choir
Fa - ther– The Mes - si - ah.
Unison
mf
The Mes - si - ah. Bless - ed
mf
B
F♯
F♯m
F♯m
E
E
D

146
day in the house of Da - vid;
146
F♯m
mf
E
D M7
150
Born a King, Lord of lords, Son of
E
D
150
F♯m
E
God. Bless - ed
D M7
E
D

154 *Divisi*

mel.

Child, He was born to save us,

F♯m E D M7

E/D

158

Prince of Peace, Mighty - y

F♯m

CD: 33

cresc.

f

God, the Mes - si - ah. The Mes -

cresc.

f

E D M7 E/D

cresc.

162 *Student (or young adult) Solo*

f

Lord of lords, Son of God, Prince of Peace, Might-y

si - ah, The Mes - si - ah,

162 F♯m B/F♯ F♯m

f

God, The Mes - si - ah.

166

He is the Mes-

B/F♯ 166 Gm

170
He's the Won-der - ful Coun - sel - or, He's the In - fi - nite
si - ah. The Mes - si - ah,
G m
C
G
170
G m
CD: 34
Soloist may sing melody with choir
Fa - ther– The Mes - si - ah.
Unison mf
The Mes - si - ah. Bless - ed
Unison mf
C
G
G m
G m
F
F
E♭

174
day in the house of Da - vid;
174
Gm
F
E♭M7
mf
178
Born a King, Lord of lords, Son of
F/E♭
178
Gm
F
God. Bless - ed
E♭M7
F/E♭

182
Divisi
mel.
Child, He was born to save us,
182
Gm
F
E♭M7
186
Prince of Peace, Mighty
F
E♭
186
Gm
cresc.
f
God, the Mes - si - ah. The Mes-
cresc.
f
F
E♭M7
F
E♭
cresc.

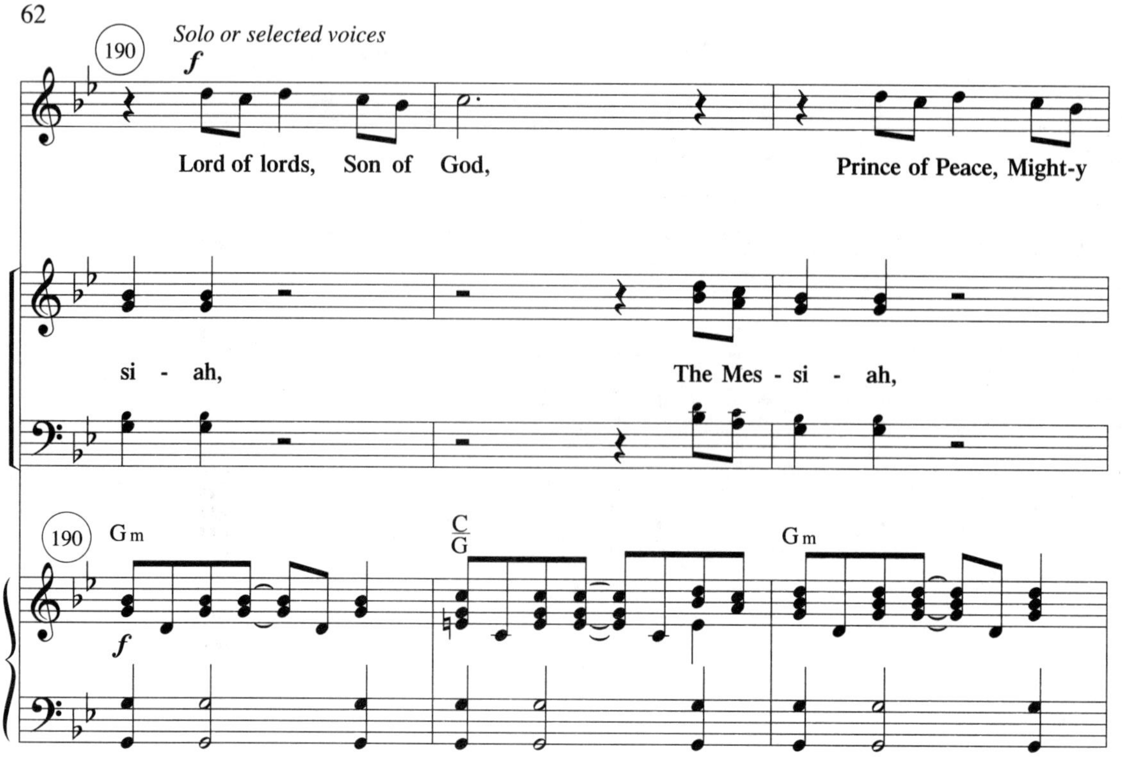

190

Solo or selected voices

f

Lord of lords, Son of God, Prince of Peace, Might-y

si - ah, The Mes - si - ah,

190 Gm

f

C/G

Gm

194

cresc.

God, The Mes - si - ah.

cresc.

The Mes - si - ah.

cresc.

C/G

194 G

cresc.

IV
Shine Your Light of Love

Adult Choir, Children's Choir, Child Solo and Narrator

Arranged by Tom Fettke

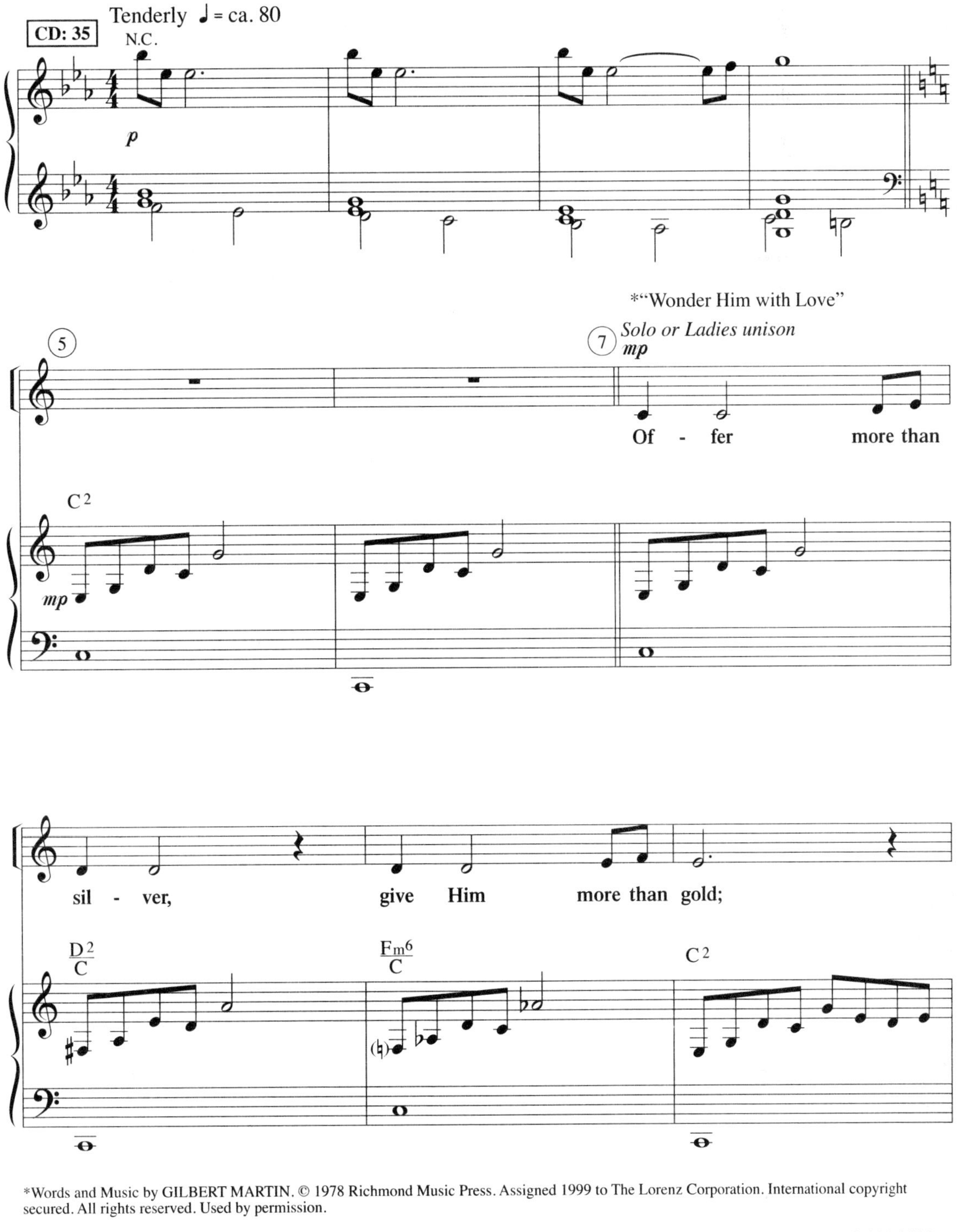

CD: 35

Tenderly ♩ = ca. 80

N.C.

p

*"Wonder Him with Love"

5

C2

mp

7

Solo or Ladies unison

mp

Of - fer more than

11
Vel - vet won't be need - ed sleep - ing in this
C/B♭
F2/A
Fm2/A♭
15
cold. Spin no silk - en lac - es
F/G
G/F
E♭
Fm7/4
19
whit - er than the dove. Rath - er, plea - sure Him,
A♭m6/B♭
B°7
C2
C/B
Am7
Am7/G
CD: 36
daz - zle Him, won - der Him with love.
FM9
C6/E
Dm7/4
F/G
A♭M7

24
a tempo
rit.
Unison mp
Cat - tle gen-tly low - ing,
Unison mp
G sus
G
C2
D2/C
rit.
a tempo
28
an - gels sing on high;
Ech - oes all a -
Fm6/C
C2
C/B♭
round Him weave a lul-la - by.
F2/A
Fm2/A♭
F2/G
G/F

32
Divisi
from a -
Words need not be spo - ken, sweet songs from a -
Divisi
E♭
Fm4 7
A♭m6 / B♭
B°7
bove.
Simp - ly
36
bove.
Plea - sure Him,
daz - zle Him,
C2
C / B
Am7
C / G
FM9
C / E
CD: 37
rit.
won - der Him with love.
Dm4 7
F / G
A♭M7
G sus
G
cresc.
rit.

41
Unison
mf
Three trea - sured gifts re - flect the light,
Unison mf
41
C M7
Dm4 7
mf
cresc.
Divisi
f
One lin-g'ring star holds back the night.
cresc.
Divisi
f
C2 E
Am F♯
cresc.
f
46
Unison
mp
But what to of - fer? How shall we serve Him?
Unison mp
46
Am F♯
C2 G
F6 G
C2 G
mp

50
What spe - cial gift to bring this
F6/G
A♭M7
Gm7
new - born King?
CD: 38
rit.
Fm9
A♭M7/B♭
A♭/B♭
B♭
rit.
56
a tempo
Of - fer more than sil - ver, give Him more than
E♭2
F2/E♭
A♭m6/E♭
a tempo

60

gold; Vel - vet won't be need - ed

E♭2 60 E♭/D♭ A♭2/C

sleep - ing in this cold. 64 *mf* Spin no silk - en

mf

A♭m2/C♭ A♭2/B♭ B♭/A♭ 64 G♭

cresc. *mf*

lac - es whit - er than the dove. Rath - er,

A♭m7/4 C♭m6/D♭ D°7 E♭2 E♭/D

68
plea-sure Him,
daz-zle Him,
won-der Him with
Cm7
E♭/B♭
A♭M9
E♭/G
Fm4 7
A♭/B♭
rit.
72
Slower, freely
mp
love.
Plea-sure Him,
daz-zle Him,
C♭M7
E♭2/B♭
A♭2
E♭2/G
rit. decresc.
mp Slower, freely
rit.
76
a tempo
won-der Him
with
love.
Fm4 7
A♭2/B♭
E♭2
rit.
a tempo

**NARRATOR: When Mary saw Jesus for the first time, the memory of a painful childbirth was replaced by the memory of a promise: "the holy child born to you will be called the Son of God." *(Luke 1:35, paraphrase)*. The significance of the moment was overwhelming. The baby she cradled in her arms was a gift from God the Father…a gift of love.

For Mary, the dark and chilly stable was transformed into a place of light and warmth and worship. She worshipped the Messiah who was the embodiment of God's love…who would be made humble…who would bleed and suffer and die for the sins of all mankind.

*Music by TOM FETTKE, WILLIAM J. KIRKPATRICK and JOHN STAINER.

As we light this third candle, remember the words Jesus spoke to His disciples in the last hours of His life. "Greater love has no one than this that he lay down his life for his friends;…love each other as I have loved you." *(John 15:12-13)*

If candle light ceremony is not used, substitute this paragraph:

As we ponder God's love, remember His Son's words spoken to His disciples in the last hours of His life. "Greater love has no one than this that he lay down his life for his friends;…love each other as I have loved you." *(John 15:12-13)*

*Words, Anonymous; Music by TOM FETTKE.

CD: 41
rit.
118
Much faster ♩ = ca. 132
Love is yours and love is mine.
D/A Em/A G/A D/A G/A A D Em/A
rit.
Much faster
DM7 Em/A D Em/A DM7 Em/A
*"Christmas Is All About Love"
122
Children's Choir
mf
Christ - mas is all a - bout love, Love of the Fa - ther
D A7 D G D/F♯
mf
from a - bove. Christ - mas is all a - bout peace and joy,
126
Em A7 D A7 D A/C♯ Bm Bm/A

CD: 42 / 44
1st / 2nd time
130
Hope and life for - ev - er.
1. God wants to give you His
2. God wants to give you His
G GM7 A A6 D G A/G
on - ly Son; Reach out for the gift of God. Reach
on - ly Son; Have faith in the Son of God. Have
D/F♯ Bm Em7 G/A A D
134
out, reach out for the gift of God; Reach
faith, have faith in the Son of God; Have
G A/G D/F♯ D Bm7
out for the gift of God.
faith in the Son of
1
Em7 G/A A7 D Em/A DM7 Em/A

CD: 43
(to pg. 74, meas. 122)
2
God.
D
Em
A
D M7
Em
A
D
Em
A
D M7
Em
A
CD: 45
E♭
Fm
B♭
E♭M7
Fm
B♭
146
f
Christ - mas is all a - bout love, Love of the Fa - ther
E♭
B♭7
E♭
A♭
E♭
G
f
from a - bove. Christ - mas is all a - bout peace and joy,
150
Fm
B♭7
E♭
B♭7
E♭
B♭
D
Cm
Cm
B♭

CD: 46
154
Hope and life for - ev - er. Love, peace,
A♭ A♭M7 B♭ B♭6 E♭ Fm/B♭
joy, hope; Love, peace, joy, hope,
E♭M7 Fm/B♭ E♭ Fm/B♭ E♭M7 Fm/B♭
158
Life for - ev - er and ev - er. Hal - le - lu - jah!
E♭ Fm/B♭ E♭M7 Fm/B♭ E♭
ff
Hal - le - lu - jah!
A♭/B♭ E♭
ff

V
Shine Your Light of Joy

Adult Choir, 2 Adult Soloists, Narrator

Arranged by Tom Fettke

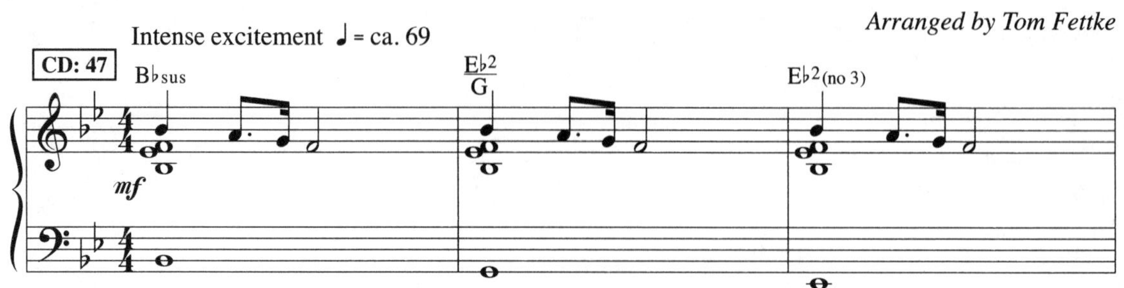

10

shine, There un-fold-ing in the

B♭2/D Cm7

CD: 48

heav-ens The mo-ment in time.

B♭2/D Fsus/E♭ Fsus F

14

mf

1. When God's love lit up the night sky,
2. As the King left Heav-en's glo-ry

Choir
mf

Oo

mf

14

E♭2/G B♭/F

mf

You could hear the an - gels sing.
An - gels sang with thun - d'rous praise.
Oo
E♭2
F7sus
F
18
They an-nounced the birth of Je - sus, The
Now let's join the an - gel cho - rus; Ex -
Ah
A♭
E♭/G

cresc.

King of all kings.
alt - ing His name!

cresc.

f

Nev - er - end - ing

cresc.

f

E♭/F F E♭/F F E♭/F F

cresc.

22

f

Joy and praise fills the heav - ens for the

Unison

joy! Praise fills the heav - ens for the

Unison

22 B♭ F/A

f

Lord of lords___for - ev - er reigns. Nev - er - end - ing

Lord of lords___for - ev - er reigns. Nev - er - end - ing

Gm Gm/F C/E E♭/F F E♭/F F

26

joy! Je - sus is___our Sav - ior and

Divisi

joy! Je - sus is___our Sav - ior and

Divisi

26

B♭ F/A F/G D/F♯

CD: 50
2nd time
Lord! We will re - joice in
Lord! We will re - joice in
Gm
Cm
Gm/B♭
A♭
Fm7
1
nev - er - end - ing, nev - er - end - ing
nev - er - end - ing, nev - er - end - ing
1
G♭
A♭
G♭/B♭
A♭

CD: 49 decresc.

(to pg. 79, meas. 14) 2

joy. nev - er-end - ing

decresc.

joy. nev - er-end - ing

decresc.

B♭2 (to pg. 79, meas. 14) 2 G♭ A♭

35 *"Joy to the World"

joy!

joy to the earth! The Sav - ior reigns! Let men their songs em -

B♭ Gm7 Cm7 B♭/F D7/F♯ Gm B♭/F E♭ Dm7

*Words by ISAAC WATTS; Music by GEORGE FREDERICK HANDEL. Arr. © 2003 by Pilot Point Music (ASCAP). All rights reserved. Administered by The Copyright Company, 1025 16th Avenue South, Nashville, TN 37212.

mf
39
ploy, While fields and floods, rocks,
Unison mf
Cm7
F7sus
B♭
hills and plains Repeat the sound-ing joy, Re-
Unison
Gm7
E♭M7
Dm7
CD: 51
cresc.
Divisi
peat the sound-ing joy, Re-peat, re-peat the
Cm7
F7
D/F♯
Gm
Cm7
B♭/D
E♭m6/G♭
cresc.

45
f
sound - ing joy! Praise fills the
B♭/F D/F♯ G G/F C/E Dm7 C
Unison
heav - ens for the King of kings for - ev - er
G/B Am Am/G
49
Divisi
reigns. Nev - er - end - ing joy! Je - sus is our
D/F♯ F/G G F/G G C

CD: 52

Sav - ior and Lord! We will re - joice with

G/B G/A E/G♯ Am Dm Am/C B♭ F6/A G G/F

53

Unison

joy! Praise fills the heav - ens for the

Unison

C/E Dm7 C G/B

King of kings for - ev - er reigns. Nev - er - end - ing

Am Am/G D/F♯ F/G G F/G G

57
Divisi
joy! Je - sus is our Sav - ior and
Divisi
C
G B
G A
E G♯
Unison
sub. mf
Lord! We will re - joice in
Unison
sub. mf
Am
Dm
Am C
B♭
decresc.
61
cresc. poco a poco
Divisi
nev - er - end - ing, nev - er - end - ing, nev - er - end - ing,
cresc. poco a poco
Divisi
A♭
B♭
A♭ C
B♭
A♭
Gm7
mf cresc. poco a poco

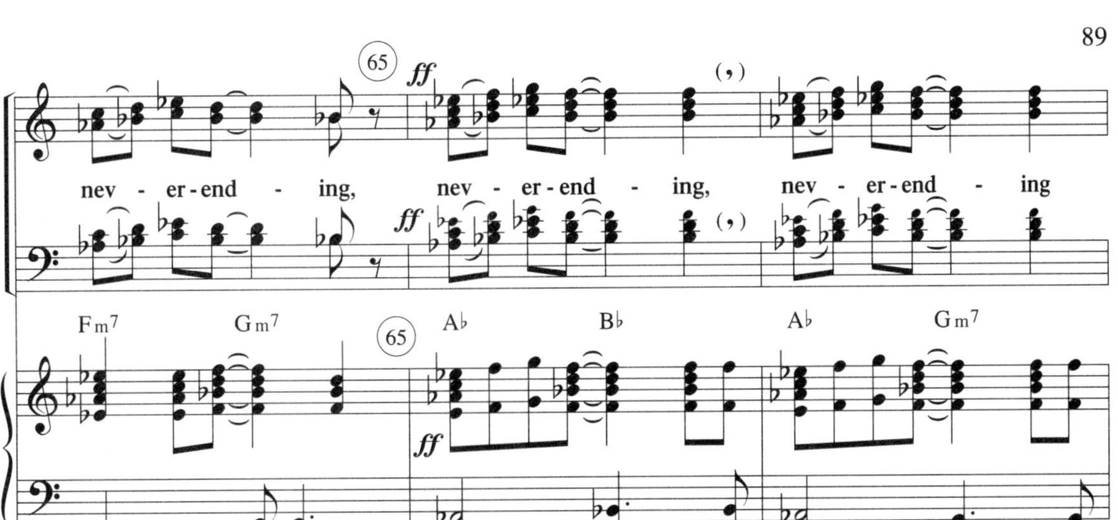

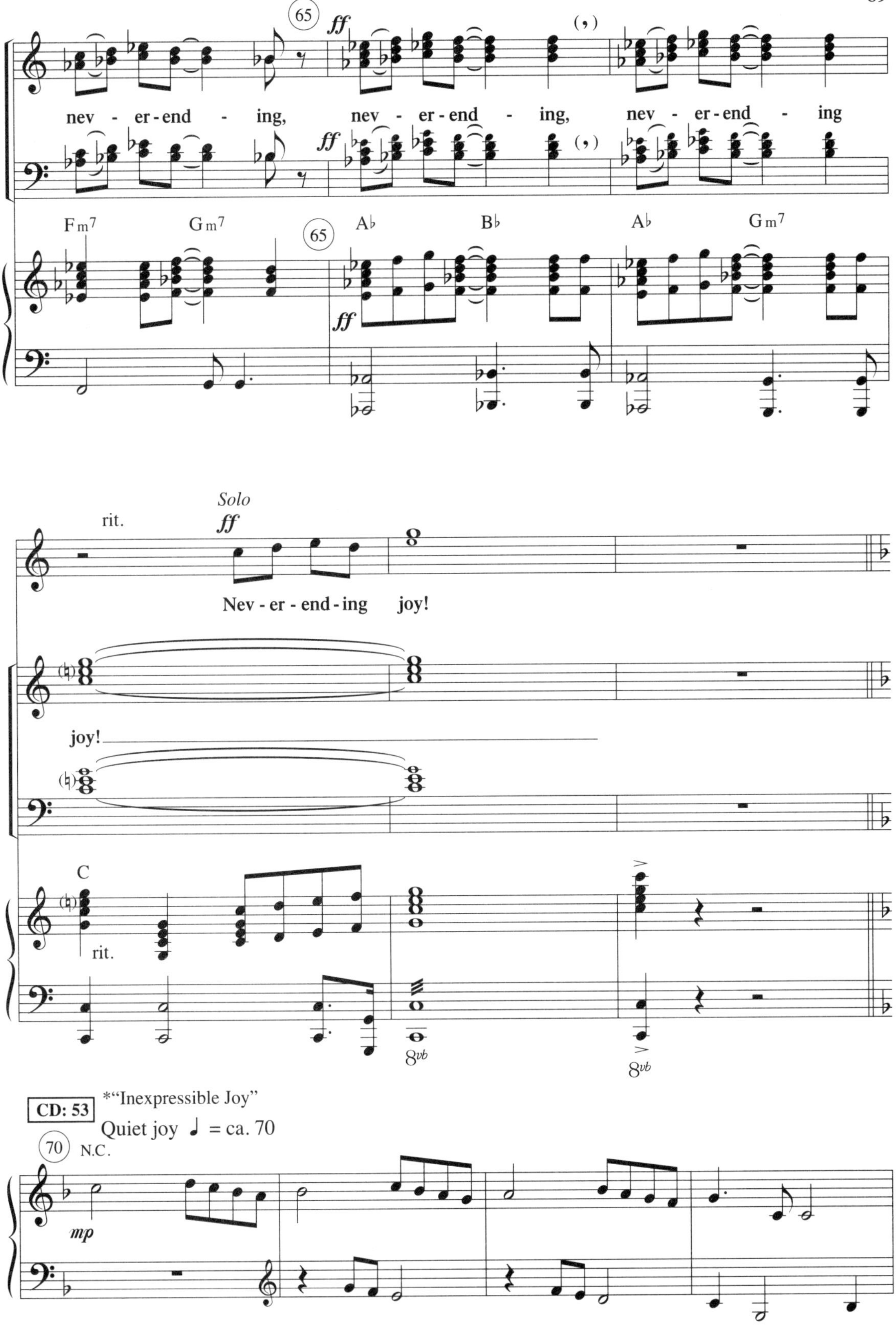
65
ff
(,)
nev - er-end - ing, nev - er-end - ing, nev - er-end - ing
Fm7
Gm7
A♭
B♭
A♭
Gm7
rit.
Solo
Nev - er - end - ing joy!
joy!
C
8vb
CD: 53
*"Inexpressible Joy"
Quiet joy ♩ = ca. 70
70
N.C.
mp

*Music by TOM FETTKE and Traditional French Carol.

*NARRATOR: When Jesus was born, what was the response from earth and heaven? The whole universe celebrated with exuberant joy… passionate joy…triumphant joy. Mary, Joseph, the angels, the shepherds, all responded with spontaneous, wide-eyed, inexpressible joy. They couldn't keep it to themselves; after all, the long-awaited Messiah was here.

When we read of the Magi, we sense the anticipation that compelled them to follow a star for those countless miles. They came for the joy of seeing and worshipping the King of kings and Lord of lords. When they entered God's presence, they experienced the fullness of joy.

As we light this fourth candle, remember the joy of your salvation and the unending joy of God's presence. "You will go out in joy and be led forth in peace; the mountains and hills will burst into song before you, and all the trees of the field will clap their hands." *(Isaiah 55:12)*

If the candle lighting ceremony is not used, substitute this paragraph:

As we celebrate this Christmas, remember the joy of your salvation. Remember the unending joy of God's presence. "You will go out in joy and be led forth in peace; the mountains and hills will burst into song before you, and all the trees of the field will clap their hands." *(Isaiah 55:12)*

89
93
97
CD: 54
Jubilantly ♩ = ca. 92
103
mf
E♭(no 3)
E♭(no 3)/B♭
E♭(no 3)/A♭
E♭(no 3)
E♭(no 3)/C
E♭(no 3)/B♭
E♭(no 3)
E♭(no 3)/B♭
E♭(no 3)/A♭
E♭(no 3)
E♭(no 3)/C
E♭(no 3)/B♭

*Words by WAYNE BOOSAHDA and STEPHANIE BOOSAHDA; Music by STEPHANIE BOOSAHDA.

Unison
Thro' His ho - ly vir - gin birth.
Ju - bi - la - te De - o.
Eb/G
Cm
Eb(no 3)
Ebsus
Eb
Bb/Eb
Eb
115
Ju - bi - la - te De - o.
Ju-bi-la, ju-bi-la - te De - o.
115
Eb(no 3)
Ebsus
Eb
Bb/Eb
Eb(no 3)
Eb(no 3)/Bb
Eb(no 3)/Ab
CD: 55
Ju-bi-la, ju-bi-la - te De - o.
Ju-bi-la, ju-bi-la - te De - o.
Eb(no 3)
Eb(no 3)/C
Eb(no 3)/Bb
Eb(no 3)
Eb(no 3)/Bb
Eb(no 3)/Ab

120
Ju-bi-la, ju-bi-la - te De - o.
Je - sus, the In - car - nate Word,
Eb(no 3)
Eb(no 3)
C
Eb(no 3)
Bb
120
Eb(no 3)
Ju - bi - la - te De - o.
Bro't good news to all who heard.
Eb(no 3) Ebsus Eb Eb2 Eb
Eb(no 3)
124
Divisi
Ju - bi - la - te De - o.
Healed the lep - er, blind and lame,
Eb(no 3) Ebsus Eb
Bb
Eb
Eb(no 3)
124
Ab

Unison
Ju - bi - la - te De - o.
All who called up - on His name.
A♭ F m7 E♭/B♭ B♭ E♭/G C m
Ju - bi - la - te De - o. Ju - bi - la - te De - o.
E♭(no 3) E♭sus E♭ B♭/E♭ E♭ E♭(no 3) E♭sus E♭ B♭/E♭ E♭(no 3)
129
Ju - bi - la, ju - bi - la - te De - o. Ju - bi - la, ju - bi - la - te De - o.
129
F(no 3) F(no 3)/C F(no 3)/B♭ F(no 3) F(no 3)/D F(no 3)/C

CD: 56
Ju-bi-la, ju-bi-la - te De - o. Ju-bi-la, ju-bi-la - te De - o.
F(no 3)
F(no 3) C
F(no 3) B♭
F(no 3)
F(no 3) D
F(no 3) C
133
He was slain and cru - ci - fied,
Ju - bi - la - te De - o.
F(no 3)
Fsus F F2 F
For our sins He bled and died
Divisi
Ju - bi - la - te De - o.
F(no 3)
Fsus F C F(no 3)

137
Ju - bi - la - te De - o.
To a - tone for A - dam's race.
137
B♭
Gm7
F/C
C
CD: 57
cresc.
Gave His life and took our place.
Ju - bi - la - te De - o.
Unison
cresc.
F/A
Dm
F(no 3)
Fsus
F
C/F
F
cresc.
142
f
Divisi
Ju - bi - la - te De - o.
Laid to rest in Jo - seph's tomb,
f
Divisi
F(no 3)
Fsus
F
C
F(no 3)
142
G(no 3)
f

Con - quered death in earth's dark womb.
G(no 3)
146
Keys of death and hell in hand,
G(no 3)
146
C
Unison
Christ the Vic - tor rose a - gain.
Keys of death in hand.
C
Bm7
Am7
D
G
B
Em7

Ju - bi - la - te De - o. Ju - bi - la - te De - o.
Unison
G(no 3) G sus G D/G G G sus G D/G G(no 3)
151
Ju-bi-la, ju-bi-la - te De - o. Ju-bi-la, ju-bi-la - te De - o.
Divisi
151
A♭(no 3) A♭(no 3)/E♭ A♭(no 3)/D♭ A♭(no 3) A♭(no 3)/F A♭(no 3)/E♭
CD: 58
Ju-bi-la, ju-bi-la - te De - o. Ju-bi-la, ju-bi-la - te De - o.
A♭(no 3) A♭(no 3)/E♭ A♭(no 3)/D♭ A♭(no 3) A♭(no 3)/F A♭(no 3)/E♭

155 *Solo*

f

Praise to Him, the Ho - ly One. The

Divisi

Ju - bi - la - te De - o.

155 A♭(no 3) A♭sus A♭ E♭/A♭ A♭

Spir - it and the Bride say, "Come!'

Ju - bi - la - te De - o.

A♭(no 3) A♭sus A♭ E♭ A♭(no 3)

159
In the clouds we shall as - cend
Ju - bi - la - te De - o.
159
D♭
B♭m
A♭/E♭
E♭
Ev - er - more to reign with Him.
Ju - bi - la - te De - o.

A♭/C
Fm
A♭
A♭sus
A♭
E♭/A♭
A♭

163

Ju - bi - la - te De - o. Ju - bi - la - te De - o.

163 A♭ A♭sus A♭ E♭/A♭ A♭(no 3) A♭ A♭sus A♭ E♭/A♭ A♭

167

De -

Ju - bi - la - te De - o. Ju - bi - la - te De - o.

A♭ D♭/A♭ A♭ D♭ E♭ Fm D♭M7 Cm7 D♭ E♭ D♭/F E♭ 167 A♭(no 3)

CD: 59
o.
A♭(no 3)
171
Unison mf
Ju-bi-la, ju-bi-la-te De-o. Ju-bi-la, ju-bi-la-te De-o.
mf
A♭(no 3)
A♭(no 3)/E♭
A♭(no 3)/D♭
A♭(no 3)
A♭(no 3)/F
E♭
A♭/E♭
mf

Ju-bi-la, ju-bi-la - te De - o. Ju-bi-la, ju-bi-la - te De - o.
A♭(no 3) A♭(no 3)/E♭ A♭(no 3)/D♭ A♭(no 3) A♭(no 3)/F E♭ A♭/E♭
175
f
Ju - bi - la - te,
f
Ju-bi-la, ju-bi-la - te De - o. Ju-bi-la, ju-bi-la - te De - o.
f
175
A♭(no 3) A♭(no 3)/E♭ A♭(no 3)/D♭ A♭(no 3) A♭(no 3)/F E♭ A♭/E♭
f

Ju - bi - la - te
Ju-bi-la, ju-bi-la - te De - o. Ju-bi-la, ju-bi-la - te De - o.
A♭(no 3) A♭(no 3)/E♭ A♭(no 3)/D♭ A♭(no 3) A♭(no 3)/F E♭ A♭/E♭
179
ff
Ju - bi - la - te De - o,
ff
Ju-bi-la, ju-bi-la - te De - o. Ju-bi-la, ju-bi-la - te De - o.
ff
179
A♭(no 3) A♭(no 3)/E♭ A♭(no 3)/D♭ A♭(no 3) A♭(no 3)/F E♭ A♭/E♭
ff

Ju - bi - la - te De - o
Ju-bi-la, ju-bi-la - te De - o. Ju-bi-la, ju-bi-la - te De - o.
A♭(no 3) A♭(no 3)/E♭ A♭(no 3)/D♭ A♭(no 3) A♭(no 3)/F E♭ A♭/E♭
185
Divisi
Ju - bi - la - te De - o.
185
A♭(no 3) A♭(no 3)/E♭ A♭(no 3)/D♭ A♭(no 3) A♭(no 3)/F E♭ A♭/E♭ A♭(no 3) A♭(no 3)/E♭ A♭(no 3)/D♭

Ju-bi-la-te De - o.
Ju-bi-la-te De - o.
Ju-bi-la-te
Ab(no 3)
Ab(no 3)/F
Eb
Ab/Eb
Ab(no 3)
Ab(no 3)/Eb
Ab(no 3)/Db
Ab(no 3)
189
De - o.
We re-joice in God!
Ab(no 3)/F
Eb
Ab/Eb
Ab(no 3)/Db
Ab(no 3)
Ab(no 3)/F
Ab(no 3)/Eb
Ab(no 3)
Ab(no 3)/F
Ab(no 3)/Eb
Ab
8va

VI
Worship the Light

Adult Choir, Senior Adult Choir, Senior Adult Soloist, Opt. Children's Choir, Child Soloist, Opt. Youth Choir, and Narrator

Arranged by Tom Fettke

*CHILD: Sometimes as I walk around during the Christmas holidays and I see things ornately decorated with lights, Santas, ribbons and bows, I think to myself, "How many of these people really know the true meaning of Christmas? How many know that on Christmas day when they're receiving all of their gifts, those gifts represent the presents that baby Jesus received from shepherds and wisemen?"

I just hope that everyone will someday understand the true meaning of Christmas.

*Words and Music by DICK and MELODIE TUNNEY.

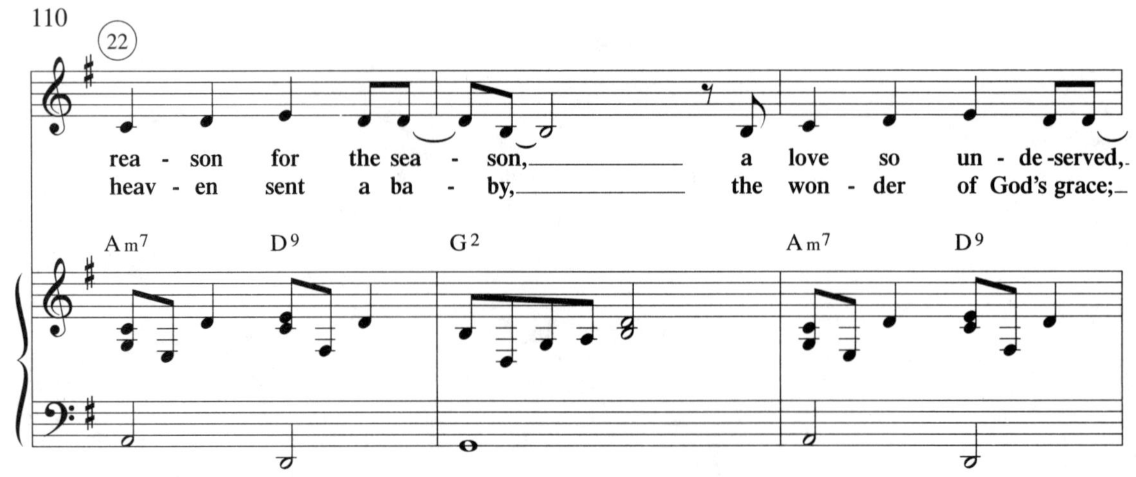
22
rea - son for the sea - son, a love so un - de-served,
heav - en sent a ba - by, the won - der of God's grace;
Am7 D9 G2 Am7 D9

26
2nd time: Both, child sings cue notes
That God sent His Son, Je - sus, as a
So with our heart a bless - ing, we
G2 Cm7 B♭/D

CD: 62 1st time
CD: 64 2nd time
Both times: Adult solo
rit.
mf
gift for all the world.
bring this wish to say.
Mer - ry
Cm/E♭ Cm7 Dsus D7
rit.

31
a tempo
Christ - mas to you, may you know true peace on
2nd time only: Children's choir, ensemble or solo
mf
Mer - ry, mer - ry Christ - mas, know true peace on
G2 G2/B C2 G2 G2/B
mf
a tempo
35
earth. May the warmth of hope sur - round you as you
earth. May hope sur - round you,
C2 Am7 G/B C2#4 C G/B
39
cel - e - brate our Sav - ior's birth. And re - mem - ber that He
cel - e - brate our Sav - ior's birth. Mer - ry, mer - ry
Am7 D7sus D G2 G2/B

came from the heart of God a - bove For
Christ - mas, heart of God, of God a-bove.
C2
G2
G2/B
A/C♯
43
true Christ - mas spir - it is found in Je -
True Christ - mas spir - it is found in
43
Am7
G2/B
C2
47
CD: 63
1st time
sus' love.
Je - sus' love.
D7
47
G2
G2/B
C2

**NARRATOR: Darkness covered all creation until God said, "Let there be light!" and there was light.

Darkness covered our hearts until God said, "Let there be light!" and there was light– a light that reaches into every dark corner of our lives.

This Christmas rejoice for Christ in us is the hope of glory.

Rejoice for in God there is perfect peace.

Rejoice in God's wonderful gift of love…Jesus.

Rejoice, for to live in God's presence is the fullness of joy.

***As we light this last candle, we complete the celebration. We lift up the truth that Jesus Christ is the Light of the World. Let's rejoice in the light of His presence as we sing together Christmas carols that express the hope, peace, love and joy found in our Lord and Savior, Jesus Christ.

If the candle lighting ceremony is not used, substitute this paragraph:

As we complete this Christmas celebration, let us lift up the truth that Jesus Christ is the Light of the World. Let's rejoice in the light of His presence as we sing together Christmas carols that express the hope, peace, love and joy found in our Lord and Savior, Jesus Christ.

*Music by TOM FETTKE and HENRY T. SMART.

***This is the main candle (no. 5). See production notes for options.

60

63

67

70

74

Segue to "Carols of Worship and Praise"

Carols of Worship and Praise

All Choirs and Congregation

Carols of Hope
O Come, All Ye Faithful*
Angels We Have Heard on High
How Great Our Joy!
Joy to the World
Angels, from the Realms of Glory
Hark! the Herald Angels Sing

Arranged by Tom Fettke

*Words to the carols for reproduction are found on page 141.

89
Car - ols of wor - ship we of - fer the King.
C
D/C
C
G/B
Bm
G/B
Am
CM7/G
D/F♯
93
Car - ols of love, Car - ols of joy,
G
D/F♯
Em
Bm
Bm7
97
CD: 67
Car - ols of praise and re - joic - ing we sing.
C
D/C
C
G/B
Bm
G/B
Am
Bm/D
D7
G

*Words, Latin Hymn, attr. to JOHN F. WADE; Music, attr. to JOHN F. WADE. Arr.

110
Divisi
CD: 68
Come and be - hold Him– born the King of
Divisi
G/B Am G Am D/F♯ G D/F♯ G Em A/C♯
Unison mp
114
Divisi mf
an - gels! O come, let us a - dore Him! O
Unison mp
mf
D C/D G D/G G G4/2 G
mp
f
118
come, let us a - dore Him! O come, let us a -
Divisi
G/D D G/D G4/2/D G/D D G/B Am G D/F♯ A7/E
mf
f

*Words and Music, Traditional French Carol. Arr.

*As in the beginning, a Senior Adult Solo may sing along with the Senior Adult Choir.

140
Car - ols of peace, Car - ols of wor - ship we
Em Bm Bm7 140 C D/C C G/B Bm G/B
144
f
of - fer the King. Car - ols of love,
f
Am CM7/G D/F♯ 144 G D/F♯
f
148
Car - ols of joy, Car - ols of praise and re -
Em Bm Bm7 148 C D/C C G/B Bm G/B

*Words and Music, Traditional German Carol. Arr.

161
Joy, joy, joy! Joy, joy, joy! Praise we the Lord in
Am G C Am G C G7/B C E7 F
CD: 72 1st time
heav'n on high! Praise we the Lord in heav'n on high!
1 (to pg. 122, meas. 153)
B°/D E7 Am C B°7 Am E7 F B°/D E7 Am
CD: 73
2
cresc.
heav'n on high!
B°/D E A

*"Joy to the World"

*Words by ISAAC WATTS; Music by GEORGE FREDERICK HANDEL.

*As in the beginning, a Senior Adult Solo may sing along with the Senior Adult Choir.

*Words by JAMES MONTGOMERY; Music by HENRY T. SMART. Arr.

200
Wing your flight o'er all the earth. Ye who sang cre - a - tion's sto - ry,
Cm/B♭ Cm B♭2 F/A B♭ 200 B♭2 D7/A
204 Divisi cresc.
Now pro - claim Mes - si - ah's birth. Come and wor - ship.
Divisi cresc.
Gm G4 2 Gm F/C C7 F 204 F/E♭
cresc.
f
Come and wor - ship. Wor - ship Christ, the new - born King.
f
B♭/D E♭ Cm7 B♭/D Cm7/E♭ E♭6 B♭/F F7 B♭
f

208
Come and wor - ship. Come and wor - ship. Wor - ship Christ, the
F F/E♭ B♭/D E♭ Cm7 B♭/D Cm7/E♭ E♭6
CD: 76
*"Hark! the Herald Angels Sing"
214
Congregation may continue
Unison
new - born King. Hark! the her - ald
B♭/F F F7 B♭ F7/C D sus D G C2/A
an - gels sing, "Glo - ry to the new - born King!
G/B CM7 C6 G/D C2 G/D D G

218
Peace on earth, and mer - cy mild– God and sin - ners
G C2/A G/B Em/C♯ A7/C♯ Bm7 Am/C D Em/G
rec - on - ciled." Joy - ful, all ye na - tions rise;
222
Divisi
D/A A7 D G/D C/D G/D D
Join the tri - umph of the skies. With th'an - gel - ic
226
G/D C/D G/D D C E7/B

host pro - claim, "Christ is born in Beth - le - hem."
Am E Am Am7 D Bm/C G/B C D7 G
230
Hark! the her - ald an - gels sing, "Glo - ry to the
230
C E7/B Am E Am Am7 D Bm/C G/B
CD: 77
235
new - born King." Glo -
C D E♭
235
A♭ A♭/G♭ F

- - - - - ri - a
B♭m
B♭m/A♭
E♭/G
A♭
A♭/G♭
D♭/F
D♭m/F♭
E♭sus
E♭
241
in ex - cel - sis De - o! Glo -
A♭
E♭/G
Fm
D♭
A♭/E♭
E♭
241
A♭
A♭/G♭
F
- - - - - ri - a
B♭m
B♭m/A♭
E♭/G
A♭
A♭/G♭
D♭/F
D♭m/F♭
E♭sus
E♭

245
248
Choirs only
ff
in ex - cel - sis De - o! Al - le -
ff
A♭
E♭
G
Fm
D♭
A♭
E♭
E♭
A♭
B♭m
D♭
F 7
C
ff
lu - ia! Glo - ry to God!
B♭m
A♭
E♭
E♭sus
E♭
A♭
8vb
A♭
(8vb)

Father of Lights

with

Hallelujah Chorus

Words and Music by
TOM FETTKE
Arranged by Tom Fettke

With excitement ♩ = ca. 126

CD: 78
A♭/E♭
*Narration begins
p
D♭/E♭ E♭ D♭/E♭ E♭
4
A♭
mp

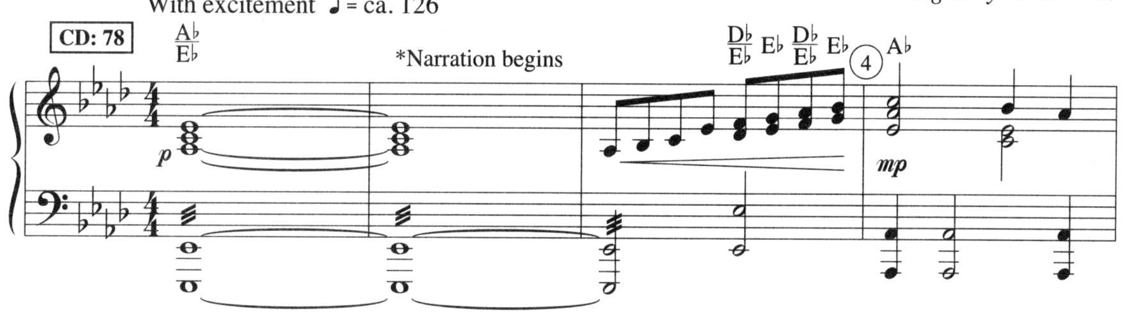

*PASTOR or NARRATOR: May the God of hope fill you with all joy, love and peace as you trust in Him. And to God our Savior be glory, majesty, power and authority through Jesus Christ, the Light of the World. Amen…and have a blessed Christmas.

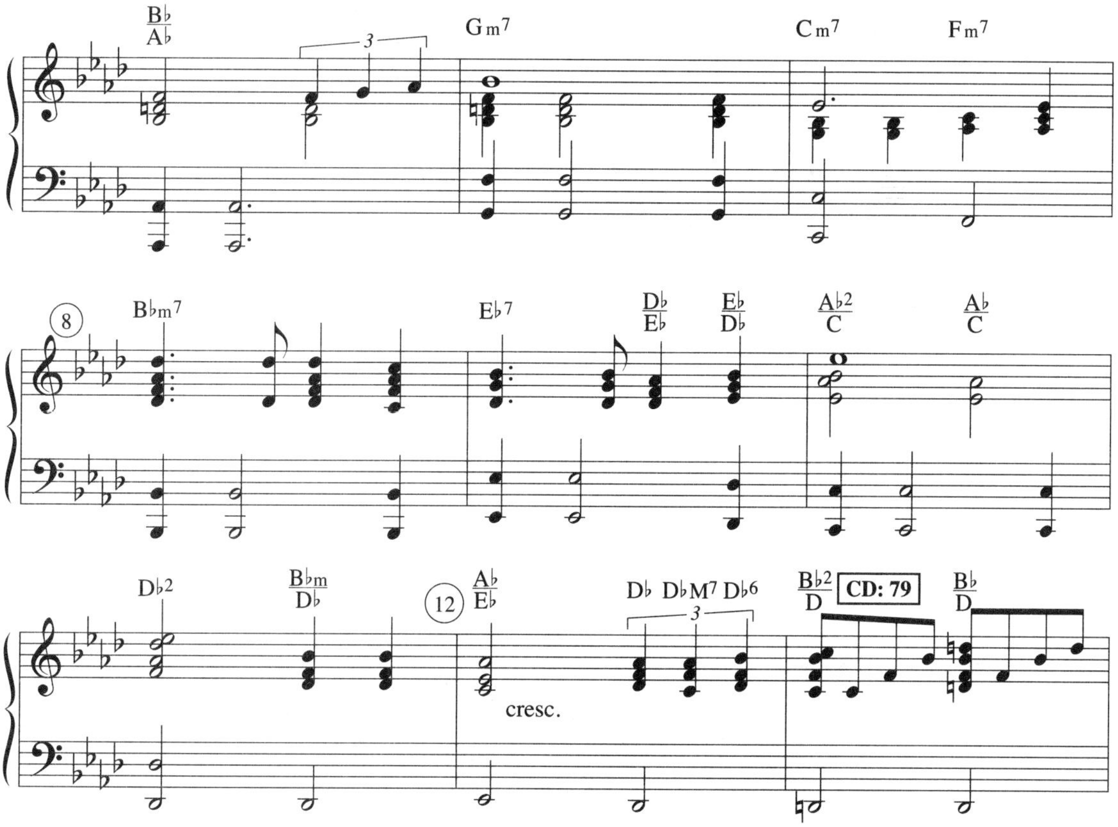
B♭/A♭
3
Gm7
Cm7
Fm7
8
B♭m7
E♭7
D♭/E♭
E♭/D♭
A♭2/C
A♭/C
D♭2
B♭m/D♭
12
A♭/E♭
cresc.
D♭ D♭M7 D♭6
3
B♭2/D
CD: 79
B♭/D

f
16
He is the
Fa-ther of lights,
Fa-ther of lights, He is the
E♭sus
E♭
D♭/A♭ A♭ D♭6/A♭ A♭
The Fa-ther of lights,
He is the
great Cre - a - tor.
The u - ni - verse re - veals,
D♭/A♭ A♭ B♭m/A♭ A♭
D♭ D♭M7 E♭sus E♭
20
Fa - ther of lights,
His bright - est star now shines;
For
D♭/A♭ A♭ D♭6/A♭ A♭
D♭/A♭ A♭ B♭m/A♭ A♭

CD: 80
He is the Fa - ther of the Light of the World.
D♭ A♭2/C B♭m7 E♭sus
He is the
25
Fa-ther of lights,
The
Fa-ther of lights, He is the great Cre - a - tor.
E♭
D♭/A♭ A♭ D♭6/A♭ A♭
D♭/A♭ A♭ B♭m/A♭ A♭
29
Fa-ther of lights,
He is the Fa-ther of lights,
The u-ni-verse re - veals,
His bright-est
D♭/A♭ A♭ D♭6/A♭ A♭
D♭ D♭M7 E♭sus E♭
D♭/A♭ A♭ D♭6/A♭ A♭

star now shines; For He is the Fa - ther of the
D♭/A♭ A♭ B♭m/A♭ A♭ D♭ A♭2/C
CD: 81
cresc.
Light of the World.
B♭m7 E♭13 E♭7 A♭ A♭2 A♭4/2 A♭ E♭m7 A♭
35
ff
Chil - dren of the light re - joice, Lift up your heart; lift
D♭ D♭4/2 D♭ D♭4/2 D♭ A♭/C B♭m B♭sus B♭m

*Words and Music by GEORGE FREDERICK HANDEL. Arr.

46
Kings and Lord of Lords!
ever; forever and ever. Hal-le-lu-jah! Hal-le-
Gb Db Db/F
46
lu-jah! Hal-le-lu-jah! Hal-le-lu-jah!
rit.
50
fff
Hal - le, Hal-
le - lu - jah!
Gb Db Ebm/Ab
8vb

Production Notes

By Chip Arnold

Production Options

Festival of Lights is a musical written to give churches the opportunity to include a candle lighting celebration as part of their Christmas musical presentation. The following production notes will also include options for those who choose not to incorporate the candle lighting ceremony.

Each monologue has two script options clearly marked in the script. There are opportunities in the musical for children, youth, and senior adult choirs to participate. They are all optional– the musical can be performed with only the adult choir if desired. There is also an opportunity for congregational singing of the Christmas carols in Part VI.

The Candle Lighting Service

The house lights should be dimmed or blacked out at the beginning of the musical so only the stage area is lit. Then the stage lights should fade to black. A child holding a lighted candle takes center stage to sing the opening solo. If a real candle is not used, a battery powered one will be fine. A special light should rise on the child during their solo until he/she finishes.

Following the solo, the stage lights come up and the production continues. One main candle should be lit at the beginning of the musical and be used to light all the other candles. Placement of this candle should be one of convenience for the sake of the production. If the child who sings the opening solo carries a lighted candle, when they is finished he should light a main candle placed at a convenient spot for the production. The four Advent candles could be lit from this main one. Normally the large middle candle is lit last. Another option would be for the middle candle to be lit first, then from it the four Advent candles could be lit. The choir director should choose whatever would work best for the sake of the performance.

Lighting the Advent candles should come during the appropriate narration as written in the script under the thematic headings of HOPE, PEACE, LOVE, and JOY. When it comes time to light each Advent candle, different members of the choir or biblical characters, if they are used, can do the job. Since there are children, youth, and senior adult choirs involved in this production, a member of each age group could light a different candle.

Some churches may not want to do just a single performance of FESTIVAL OF LIGHTS but spread the musical over the four Sundays in Advent, in addition to a full performance. If that is the case, the music and narration appropriate for the respective Sundays should be performed along with the lighting of a single candle.

(At the discretion of the choir director, any portions of Options 1-3 in the Non-Candle Lighting performance may be incorporated into the Candle Lighting performance.)

The Non-Candle Lighting Service

Option One: The house lights should be dimmed or blacked out at the beginning of the musical so that only the stage area is lit. The choir can remain seated or standing in position on the stage and perform the entire musical. The narrator should also be on stage beside the choir. The narrator should have a microphone for the monologues and, when possible, be enhanced with special lighting.

The narrator and choir director can decide whether or not the narrator should be in biblical costume. Regardless of the narrator's wardrobe choice, it might be nice to consider allowing the narrator to move about the stage as he delivers the monologue directly to the audience. This would require a spotlight or special stage lighting. Or, the narrator could appear inside different pools of light and deliver the monologue.

Option Two: In combination with Option One, the musical can be richly augmented by the use of visual media. There are a variety of visuals available, from slides and video to projected lyrics. Many of the film sequences would work beautifully if they were projected on a screen or multiple screens behind or above the choir as the music or monologue was performed. A similar effect can be achieved with individual slides of the biblical characters in dramatic scenes that would enhance specific moments in the music and/or monologues.

Option Three: Instead of using film or slides, the use of dramatic tableau behind scrim with special lighting would be very effective. At the appropriate moments in the musical, different living tableaus of angels or shepherds, the manger and the magi could appear during the song and/or monologue. All characters should be in biblical costume.

Set

There are no specific set requirements except for Option Three. There would need to be a special area designated as the "tableau" area where the actors in the living scenes will take their positions behind the scrim. Depending upon the tableau, it should be up to the director as to how complicated a set should be constructed and how many props should be used. For the other options there is no required set, but the stage and sanctuary could be made visually attractive with artistically draped fabric, an assortment of greenery, columns, and colorful banners.

Lighting

Festival of Lights could be presented with general sanctuary lighting. However, the ability to darken and/or spotlight areas of the stage, and to use follow spots for individual soloists and the narrator will add dramatic focus to the overall production. The choir area should have some special lighting, but it should be dimmed whenever the narrator speaks or a member of the choir has a solo.

There are times when the house lights could be brought up. If the choir director has decided to involve the audience in the Carols of Worship and Praise, then the house lights might be brought up for the congregation to feel a part of what is taking place in the story and to be able to read the words on the program or screen. Otherwise, the house lights should be completely out. If slides, overhead projections, and/or film are used, the house lights need to be darkened so the images are visible. The house lights can be brought up again if the pastor wishes to make any comments or extend an invitation.

Carols of Worship and Praise

O come, all ye faithful,
Joyful and triumphant.
O come ye, O come ye to Bethlehem.
Come and behold Him–
Born the King of angels!
O come, let us adore Him!
O come, let us adore Him!
O come, let us adore Him–
Christ, the Lord!

Gloria in excelsis Deo!
Gloria in excelsis Deo!

While by our sheep we watched at night,
Glad tidings brought an angel bright.
How great our joy! Great our joy!
Joy, joy, joy! Joy, joy, joy!
Praise we the Lord in heav'n on high!
Praise we the Lord in heav'n on high!

There shall be born, so he did say,
In Bethlehem a Child today.
How great our joy! Great our joy!
Joy, joy, joy! Joy, joy, joy!
Praise we the Lord in heav'n on high!
Praise we the Lord in heav'n on high!

Joy to the world! the Lord is come;
Let earth receive her King.
Let ev'ry heart prepare Him room,
And heav'n and nature sing,
And heav'n and nature sing,
And heav'n, and heav'n and nature sing.

Angels, from the realms of glory,
Wing your flight o'er all the earth.
Ye who sang creation's story,
Now proclaim Messiah's birth.
Come and worship. Come and worship.
Worship Christ, the newborn King.
Come and worship. Come and worship.
Worship Christ, the newborn King.

Hark! the herald angels sing,
"Glory to the newborn King!
Peace on earth, and mercy mild–
God and sinners reconciled."
Joyful, all ye nations rise;
Join the triumph of the skies.
With th'angelic host proclaim,
"Christ is born in Bethlehem."
Hark! the herald angels sing,
"Glory to the newborn King."

Gloria in excelsis Deo!
Gloria in excelsis Deo!

FESTIVAL
of LIGHTS

FESTIVAL
of LIGHTS

FESTIVAL
of LIGHTS

FESTIVAL
of LIGHTS

FESTIVAL
of LIGHTS

FESTIVAL
of LIGHTS

FESTIVAL
of LIGHTS

CONTENTS